THE BLUEST EYE

by
Toni Morrison

Student Packet

Written by
Pat Watson

Edited by
Katherine E. Martinez

Contains masters for:
- 2 Prereading Activities
- 4 Vocabulary Activities
- 1 Study Guide (5 pages)
- 5 Character Analysis Activities
- 3 Literary Analysis Activities
- 2 Comprehension Activities
- 4 Unit Quizzes
- 2 Final Tests (Two Levels)

PLUS Detailed Answer Key

Note

The Plume paperback edition of the book, published by the Penguin Group, ©1970, Afterword ©1993, was used to prepare this guide. The page references may differ in other editions.

Please note: This novel deals with sensitive, mature issues. Parts may contain profanity, sexual references, and/or descriptions of violence. Please assess the appropriateness of this book for the age level and maturity of your students prior to reading it with your class.

ISBN 1-58130-709-8

To order, contact your local school supply store, or—

Copyright 2001 by Novel Units, Inc., San Antonio, Texas. All rights reserved. No part of this publication may be reproduced, stored in a retrieval system, or transmitted in any way or by any means (electronic, mechanical, photocopying, recording, or otherwise) without prior written permission from the publisher, with the following exceptions: Photocopying of student worksheets by a teacher who purchased this publication for his/her own class is permissible. Reproduction of any part of this publication for an entire school or for a school system or for commercial sale is strictly prohibited. **Copyright infringement is a violation of Federal Law.**

Novel Units is a registered trademark of Novel Units, Inc.

Printed in the United States of America.

PAPERBACKS - BMI BOUND BOOKS
TEACHER'S GUIDES - AUDIO-VISUALS
PO BOX 800 - DAYTON, N.J. 08810-0800
Toll Free Phone 1-800-222-8100
America's Finest Educational Book Distributor
www.bmiedserv.com

Name _____

The Bluest Eye
Activity #1 • Prereading
Use Before Reading

Part One
Directions: Rate the following needs from 1 to 10, with number 1 being the most crucial to the development of self-esteem in children.

_____ Praise

_____ Physical affection

_____ Encouragement in development of talents

_____ Quality time with parent(s)

_____ Freedom to fail, with encouragement to try again

_____ Valuing a child's opinion

_____ Listening to a child's concerns

_____ Consistent, loving discipline

_____ Unconditional love

_____ Allowing a child to make decisions

Part Two
Directions: Rate the following detriments to the development of a child's self-esteem from 1 to 11, with number 1 being the most damaging.

_____ Physical abuse

_____ Criticism

_____ Ridicule

_____ Comparison with siblings or peers

_____ Degrading comments such as "stupid," "messy," or "dumb"

_____ Failure to give child time and attention

_____ Degrading child in front of peers or teachers

_____ Not enough affection

_____ Verbal put-downs

_____ Not allowing child to make decisions

_____ Parental strife; e.g., divorce or continual fighting

Name _____

The Bluest Eye
Activity #2 • Prereading
Use Before Reading

Getting the "Lay of the Land"

Directions: Prepare for reading by answering the following short-answer questions.

1. Who is the author?
   _____

2. What does the title suggest to you about the book?
   _____
   _____
   _____
   _____

3. When was the book written?
   _____

4. How many pages are there in the book?
   _____

5. Thumb through the book. Read three pages—one from near the beginning, one from near the middle, and one from near the end. What predictions do you make about the book?
   _____
   _____
   _____
   _____

6. What does the cover suggest to you about the book?
   _____
   _____
   _____
   _____

© Novel Units, Inc.   All rights reserved

Name _____

The Bluest Eye
Activity #3 • Vocabulary
Use With Preface–Page 58

melancholy (preface)	senile (14)	peripheral (17)	plaintive (21)
acridness (22)	pristine (23)	sadism (23)	soliloquies (24)
chagrined (24)	verification (31)	foists (33)	furtiveness (36)
malaise (37)	dissipation (38)	emasculations (42)	tacitly (43)
inexplicable (50)	petulant (50)	epithets (51)	covert (56)

Directions: Choose the word in each list that does NOT belong. Briefly explain your choice.

1.	melancholy	sadness	pensiveness	cheerfulness
2.	senile	vigorous	aged	infirm
3.	peripheral	outer	marginal	inside
4.	plaintive	wistful	blithe	mournful
5.	acridness	bland	sharpness	caustic
6.	pristine	primitive	recent	original
7.	sadism	malice	bondage	altruism
8.	soliloquies	dialogues	monologues	discursions
9.	chagrined	sheepish	unrepentant	abashed
10.	verification	proof	corroboration	contradiction
11.	foists	fraud	palms	straightforward
12.	furtiveness	overt	stealth	covertness
13.	malaise	lassitude	energy	lethargy
14.	dissipation	disintegration	boredom	satisfaction
15.	emasculations	mutilations	restoration	destruction
16.	tacitly	implied	verbal	unspoken
17.	inexplicable	explainable	mysterious	inscrutable
18.	petulant	irritable	amiable	peevish
19.	epithets	oversights	attributes	qualities
20.	covert	surreptitious	hidden	manifest

Name _____

The Bluest Eye
Activity #4 • Vocabulary
Use With Pages 61–93

gelid (61) genuflected (62) epiphany (63) extemporized (65)
macabre (65) mulatto (67) inviolable (84) surfeit (85)
ashen (87) unabashed (92)

Directions: Complete the following analogies.

1. EDUCATED is to TRAINED as SPOKEN is to _____.

2. CONFIDENT is to UNCERTAIN as EMBARRASSED is to _____.

3. BEAUTY is to LOVELINESS as HORROR is to _____.

4. FIERY is to BURNING as FROZEN is to _____.

5. COLORFUL is to DRAB as BRIGHT is to _____.

6. THOUGHT is to IDEA as REVELATION is to _____.

7. AFFLUENCE is to POVERTY as INADEQUATE is to _____.

8. INDOLENT is to INDUSTRIOUS as DISDAINFUL is to _____.

9. IRON is to ALLOY as PUREBLOOD is to _____.

10. IRREVERENCE is to TAUNTED as REVERENCE is to _____.

© Novel Units, Inc.   All rights reserved

Name _____

The Bluest Eye
Activity #5 • Vocabulary
Use With Pages 97–183

shards (104)   infirmity (116)   coherence (126)   virtues (128)
slovenliness (129)   prolific (136)   infallibility (137)   furtive (138)
shrouded (138)   synthesized (139)   fastidious (140)   omnipresence (143)
dysfunctional (160)   misanthrope (164)   antipathies (164)   asceticism (165)
celibacy (165)   diffident (166)   parody (167)   Anglophilia (168)
eccentricity (168)   predilection (169)   avocation (170)   poignant (174)
imbibed (182)

Directions: Your teacher will assign you one word from the list above. Turn to the page where the word appears in the novel and examine how it is used in context. Complete the word map for your word and explain the finished map to the class.

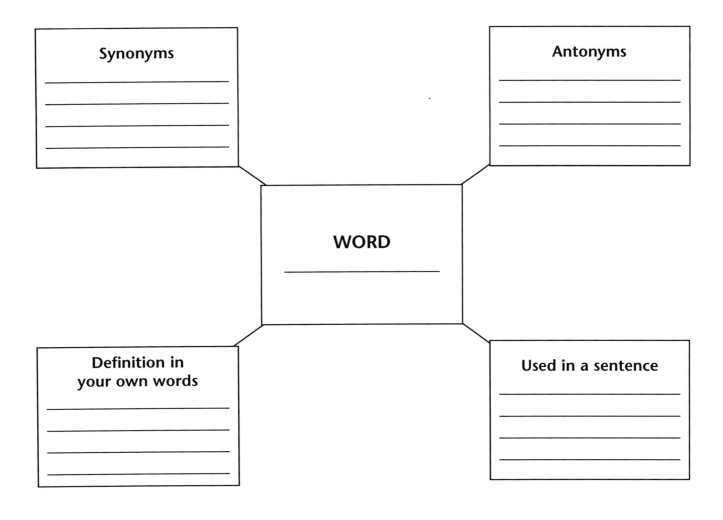

© Novel Units, Inc.   All rights reserved

Name _____

The Bluest Eye
Activity #6 • Vocabulary
Use With Pages 187–214

holocaust (187)   *Moirai* (188)   devious (191)   tendril (204)
inarticulateness (205) eloquent (205)   honed (205)   matrix (206)
volition (206)   acquiesce (206)

Directions: Match each vocabulary word with the most synonymous word or phrase.

____ 1. holocaust   a. very expressive

____ 2. *Moirai*   b. sharpened

____ 3. devious   c. consent

____ 4. tendril   d. great destruction

____ 5. inarticulateness   e. twisting strand

____ 6. eloquent   f. not straightforward

____ 7. honed   g. center; mold for casting

____ 8. matrix   h. one of the Fates

____ 9. volition   i. willing choice

____ 10. acquiesce   j. indistinct speech

Name _____

The Bluest Eye
Study Guide

Directions: Answer the following questions on a separate sheet of paper. Starred questions indicate thought or opinion questions or an activity. Use your answers in class discussions, for writing assignments, and to review for tests.

Preface–page 32

1. Identify the following: Pecola Breedlove, Claudia MacTeer, Frieda MacTeer, Cholly Breedlove, Mr. Henry, Mrs. MacTeer.
2. *How does the preface begin? Why do you think the author uses this technique?
3. *Explain the narrator's theory of why the marigolds didn't grow. Why do you think she refers to the marigolds? What does this section reveal about Pecola?
4. Why is Pecola staying with with the MacTeers? What does this reveal about Pecola's family, especially her father?
5. Why is "outdoors" to be feared? What is the difference between being put "out" and being put "outdoors"?
6. *How does Claudia react to white, blue-eyed dolls? Why do you think she reacts this way?
7. *What happens to Pecola while at the MacTeers' house? How do the sisters react? Do you think this is a typical reaction?
8. *Activity: Ask your parents or grandparents about home remedies they remember. Compare these with those Mrs. MacTeer uses (pp. 10-11). Report to the class.

Pages 33–58

1. *Describe the Breedloves' home in Lorain, Ohio. How do you think this symbolizes their lives?
2. *Quote the sentence that explains why the Breedloves live in the storefront. Which of the reasons do you think has the greatest impact on their lives?
3. Explain how each member of the Breedlove family reacts to his or her ugliness.
4. *What does Mrs. Breedlove view as her role in life? Do you think she is justified in her feelings?
5. What is the immediate cause of the fights between Cholly and Mrs. Breedlove? Explain why they "need" their fights. How do Pecola and Sammy react to their parents' fights?

Name _____

The Bluest Eye
Study Guide
page 2

6. *How does Pecola view herself? Explain how her treatment at school and by Mr. Yacobowski adds to her self-image.

7. *What is the prayer Pecola prays each night? Why is this so important to her?

8. Why are the cracks in the sidewalk and the dandelions important to Pecola?

9. Describe the three women who live above the Breedloves' storefront. What effect do they have on Pecola?

10. *Activity: Write a cinquain poem titled "Blue Eyes" reflecting Pecola's prayer for blue eyes. Pattern: Line 1: title; Line 2: two words to describe title; Line 3: three words to express action about the title; Line 4: four words to express feeling about the title; Line 5: one word that is a synonym for the title.

Pages 61–80

1. *Describe Maureen Peal and explain her effect on the school. Have you ever known anyone like her? If so, how did you react to him or her?

2. How do the boys harass Pecola? Explain their insults and the effect they have on Pecola. Who stops the harassment? How?

3. *Explain Maureen's interactions with Claudia, Frieda, and Pecola. Why do you think she befriends Pecola? What is the final outcome?

4. *How do Claudia and Frieda feel about Maureen? What do you think they mean by the "Thing" to fear?

5. Identify Mr. Henry's guests. How does he explain their presence in the MacTeers' home?

6. Why don't Claudia and Frieda tell their mother about Mr. Henry's guests?

7. *Activity: Create a montage that symbolizes Mr. MacTeer as "winter moves into his face" (p. 61).

8. *Activity: Write a five-senses poem about Envy. Pattern: Line 1: color of the emotion; Line 2: sound of the emotion; Line 3: taste of the emotion; Line 4: smell of the emotion; Line 5: sight (what the emotion looks like); Line 6: feeling evoked by the emotion.

Name _____

The Bluest Eye
Study Guide
page 3

Pages 81–93

1. Identify Geraldine and describe her lifestyle.
2. *Explain the relationship between Geraldine and her son. What effect does it have on Junior? Why is this significant to the story?
3. *What happens when Junior entices Pecola into his home? What effect does this have on Pecola? Why is this significant?
4. *Activity: Write a name poem about Pecola that describes her after she leaves Geraldine's home. Pattern: Place the letters of her name vertically on the paper. Write a descriptive word or phrase beginning with each letter.

Pages 97–109

1. What happens between Mr. Henry and Frieda? How does Frieda's father react?
2. Why do Frieda and Claudia associate Frieda's experience with Mr. Henry with the Maginot Line? Why do they involve Pecola?
3. *Describe the incident with the berry cobbler at the Fisher's home. What does this tell you about Mrs. Breedlove?
4. *Activity: Note Claudia's reaction to Frieda's physical development: "I just get tired of having everything last" (p. 100). Complete the phrase, "I just get tired..." with your own thoughts of adolescence.
5. *Activity: Draw a caricature of the Maginot Line (Miss Marie) based on the metaphors and similes about her on pages 102-103.

Pages 110–131

1. Describe Pauline (Williams) Breedlove's childhood and explain its importance to the story.
2. *Who is the "Stranger," symbolically and literally? Why is he significant to the story?
3. Describe the Breedloves' marriage at the beginning and later. What becomes its primary focus? Why?
4. Compare Pauline's "fantasy world" with the reality of her life. Include information about her love for movies.

© Novel Units, Inc.   All rights reserved

Name _____

The Bluest Eye
Study Guide
page 4

5. *How does Pauline feel about Pecola's birth, before and after? What effect do you think this has on Pecola?

6. *Activity: Write a metaphor poem about Fear based on the fear Pauline instills in her children. Pattern: Line 1: noun (subject); Lines 2-4: write something about the subject (each line should say something different and give an idea of what the subject is like); Line 5: a metaphor that begins with the title.

Pages 132–163

1. *Identify the adults in Cholly Breedlove's childhood and explain their significance. Include his mother, his father, Great Aunt Jimmy, and Blue Jack. How does Cholly's childhood affect the rest of his life?

2. What happens during Cholly's sexual encounter with Darlene? How does this affect him?

3. What does Cholly decide to do after his aunt's funeral? Why?

4. *Describe Cholly's search for and meeting with his father. Why do you think Cholly reacts as he does?

5. *Why do you think Cholly rapes Pecola? Support your answer with excerpts from the book.

Pages 164–183

1. *Identify Soaphead Church and explain his peculiarities.

2. *Who are Bertha Reese and Bob? Why are they important to the story?

3. Why is Soaphead's business "dread"?

4. What do Soaphead's business cards imply?

5. Why does Pecola come to Soaphead? How does Soaphead react? What does he tell her to do? Why? What is the result?

6. *How does the author reveal Soaphead's outlook on life? Do you think this is effective?

7. *How does Soaphead describe his relationship with Velma? How does he describe her leaving him?

8. *Activity: Write a limerick about Soaphead Church.

Name _____

The Bluest Eye
Study Guide
page 5

Pages 187–206

1. What gossip do Claudia and Frieda hear about Pecola? How do they feel about her?
2. How do Claudia and Frieda decide to "make a miracle"? Why do they do so?
3. *With whom do you think Pecola has a conversation? Who do you think this other person is? Summarize the conversation.
4. How do Claudia and Frieda react to Pecola's plight? Why?
5. *Activity: List the symptoms of Pecola's mental illness. Research to discover the correct term for this illness and the type of treatment available today. Share your findings with the class.
6. *Activity: Write name poems for Claudia and Frieda.

Pages 209–216

1. Why did Toni Morrison write *The Bluest Eye*?
2. *Do you think Morrison conveys her intended message? Why or why not?
3. *Activity: Write a critique of the novel.

Name _____

The Bluest Eye
Activity #7 • Character Analysis
Use During Reading

Attribute Web

Directions: Create an attribute web for Pecola Breedlove. As you read, feel free to add more categories of your own, additional notes, etc.

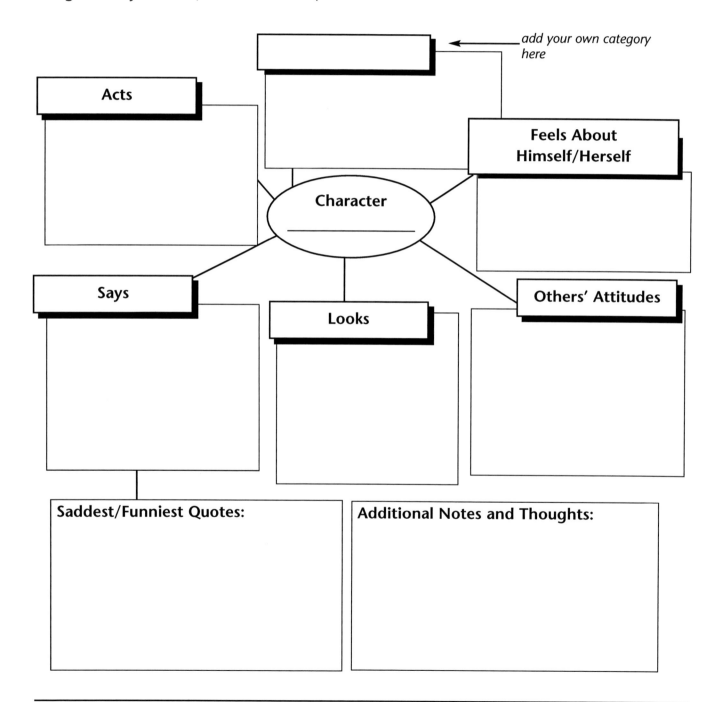

Name _____

The Bluest Eye
Activity #8 • Character Analysis
Use During Reading

Attribute Boxes

Directions: Place Cholly Breedlove's name in the center box. Record evidence about his character within the other boxes.

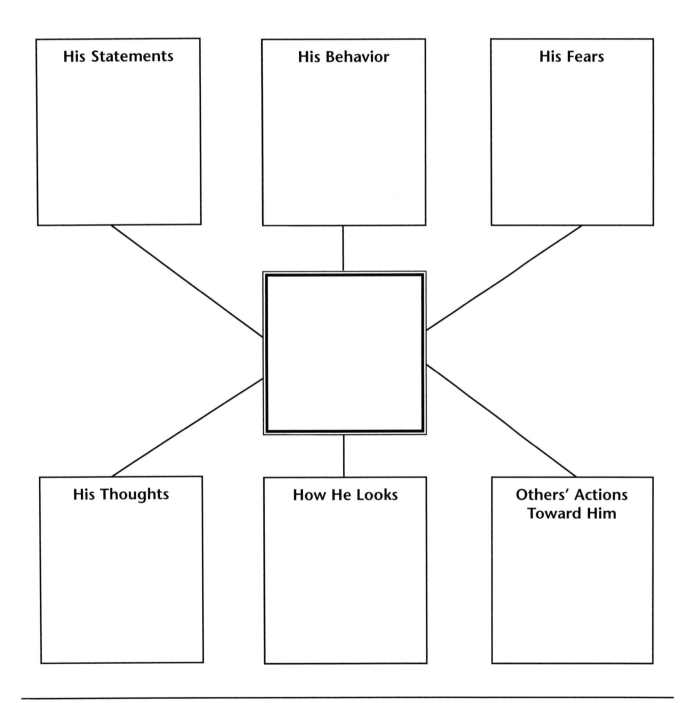

© Novel Units, Inc. All rights reserved

Name _____

The Bluest Eye
Activity #9 • Character Analysis
Use During Reading

Character Analysis

Directions: List some of the characters who appear in the novel in the boxes below. Add to this chart as more characters are introduced. Working in small groups, discuss the attributes of the various characters with other members of your group. In each character's box, write several words or phrases you feel describe him or her.

© Novel Units, Inc.

All rights reserved

Name _____

The Bluest Eye
Activity #10 • Character Analysis
Use During Reading

Sociogram

Directions: Place Pecola's name in the center circle. Add Cholly, Mrs. Breedlove, Soaphead Church, and Miss Marie in the other four circles. On the spokes surrounding each character's name, write several adjectives that describe that character. On the arrows joining one character to another, write a description of the relationship between the two characters. How does one character influence the other?

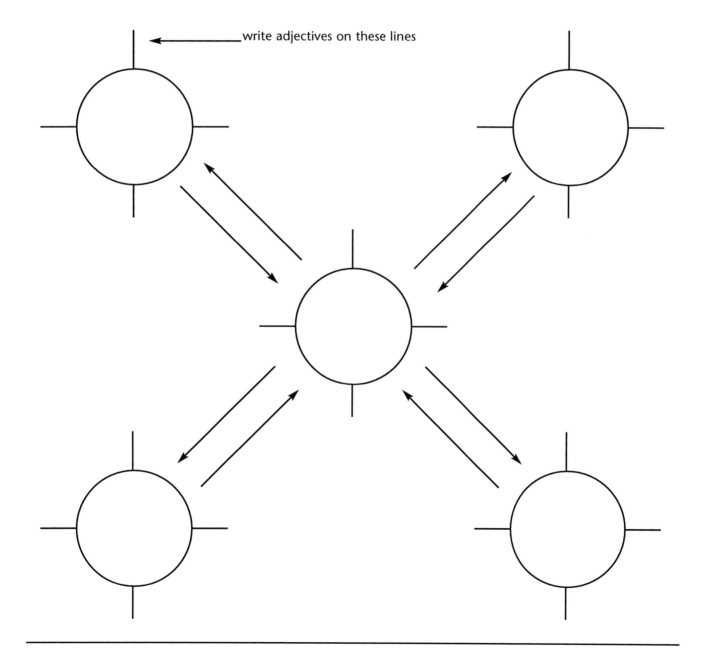

© Novel Units, Inc.

17

All rights reserved

Name _____

The Bluest Eye
Activity #11 • Character Analysis
Use During Reading

Sorting Characters

Directions: Similarities among characters are sometimes a clue to themes in the story. Place the book's characters in one or more of the groups below:

Victims	Victimizers	Fighters
Peace-lovers	**Conformists**	**Self-directors**

© Novel Units, Inc. — All rights reserved

Name _____

The Bluest Eye
Activity #12 • Story Map
Use After Reading

Story Map

Directions: Use the diagram below with a partner or small group to free associate thoughts about the novel after you have finished reading it. Jot down your thoughts in a similar format on a large piece of paper.

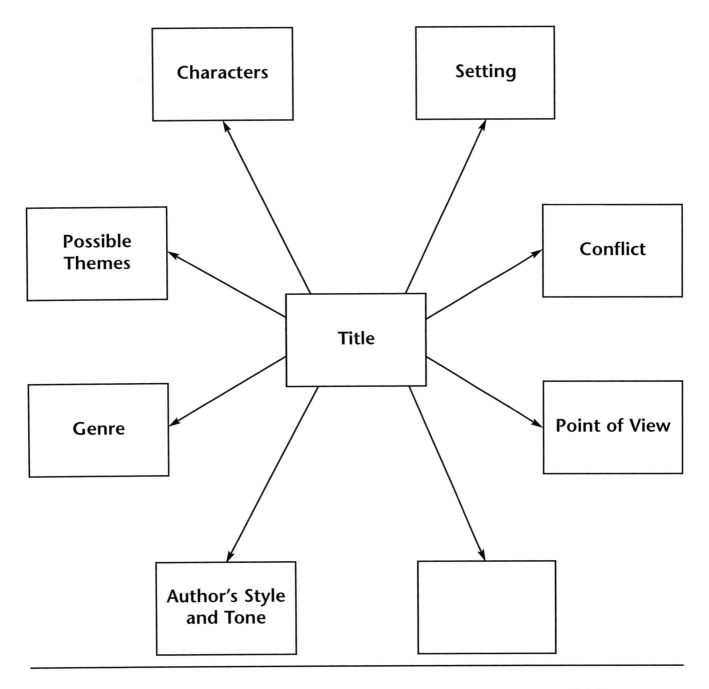

Name _____

The Bluest Eye
Activity #13 • Story Map
Use After Reading

Story Map

Directions: Select five important events from the novel and put them sequentially into this flow chart. Be sure to choose events that cover the plot through the last chapter.

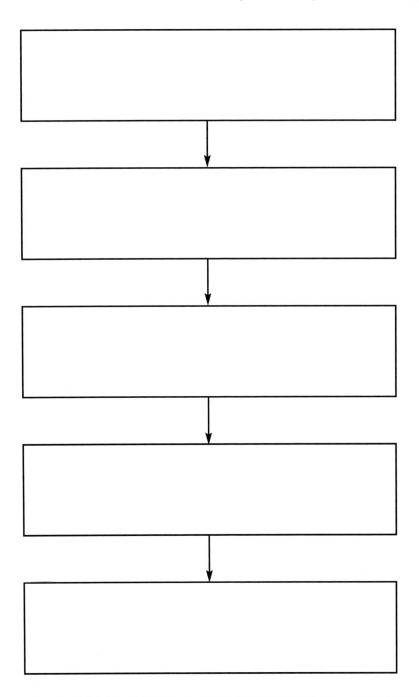

Name _____

The Bluest Eye
Activity #14 • Literary Analysis
Use After Reading

Thematic Analysis

Directions: Choose a theme from the book to be the focus of your word web. Complete the web and then answer the question in each starred box.

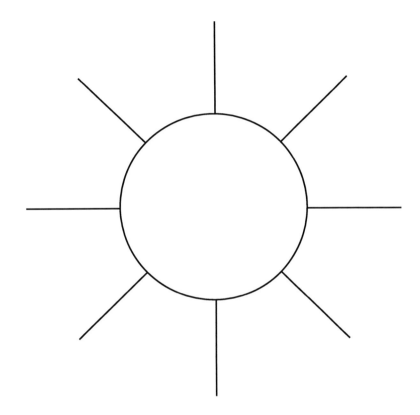

★ What is the author's main message?

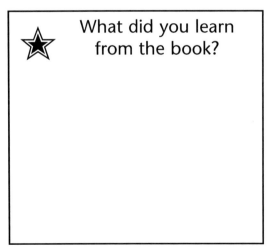

★ What did you learn from the book?

© Novel Units, Inc. All rights reserved

Name _____

The Bluest Eye
Activity #15 • Comprehension
Use After Reading

Cause-Effect

Directions: To plot cause and effect in a story, first list the sequence of events. Then mark causes with a C and effects with an E. Sometimes in a chain of events, one item may be both a cause and an effect. Draw arrows from cause statements to the appropriate effects.

Events in the story:

1.
2.
3.
4.
5.
6.
7.
8.
9.
10.

Another way to map cause and effect is to look for an effect and then backtrack to the single or multiple causes.

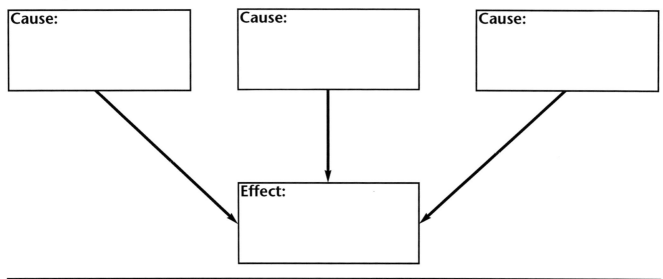

© Novel Units, Inc.   All rights reserved

Name _____

The Bluest Eye
Activity #16 • Comprehension
Use After Reading

Fishbone Map

Directions: List the effect (or result) in the box. Consider the causes. List cause 1, 2, 3, 4 (as appropriate). Add details to support the causes you list.

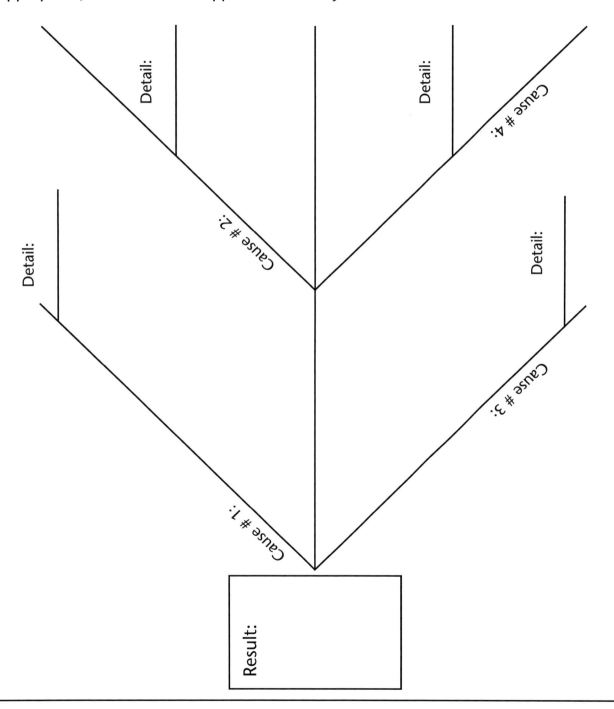

Name _____

The Bluest Eye
Activity #17 • Quiz 1
Use After Reading Pages 9–58

True/False

____ 1. Claudia's mother is cruel and abusive.

____ 2. Claudia hates her white, blue-eyed dolls.

____ 3. Claudia and Frieda go to their mother for help when Pecola starts her menstrual period.

____ 4. Cholly and Mrs. Breedlove's fights do not affect their children.

____ 5. Mr. Yacobowski treats Pecola with contempt.

____ 6. The three prostitutes hate men.

Fill in the blanks.

7. The narrator believes the marigolds fail to grow because _____ _____.

8. Pecola needs a place to stay because _____.

9. _____ comes to live with the MacTeers as a roomer.

10. Pecola believes everything will be better if _____.

11. Name the three prostitutes: _____.

Name _____

The Bluest Eye
Activity #18 • Quiz 2
Use After Reading Pages 61–93

Fill in the blanks.

1. _____ seems to befriend Pecola but then mistreats her.

2. _____ and _____ are visiting Mr. Henry when the MacTeer girls return home.

3. _____ is representative of a thrifty, mannerly, passionless black woman.

4. Junior first encounters Pecola _____.

5. Pecola reminds Geraldine of _____
_____.

Write brief answers to the following questions.

6. How does the group of boys harass Pecola?

7. How does Junior's mother react to him?

8. Why does Junior hate his mother's cat?

9. What happens when Pecola walks close to Junior's house?

10. How does Mr. Henry explain the presence of his visitors to Claudia and Frieda?

© Novel Units, Inc.   All rights reserved

Name _____

The Bluest Eye
Activity #19 • Quiz 3
Use After Reading Pages 97–183

True/False

____ 1. Pecola's mother treats her employer's little girl harshly.

____ 2. Mrs. Breedlove blames the death of her dreams on her lame foot.

____ 3. Cholly and Pauline Breedlove love each other when they marry.

____ 4. Pauline Breedlove believes Pecola is a beautiful child.

____ 5. Going to the movies makes Pauline dissatisfied with her own life.

____ 6. After the children come, the Breedloves never find pleasure in their marriage.

____ 7. Cholly's great aunt raises him after his mother abandons him.

____ 8. Cholly feels more rejection when he finds his father.

____ 9. Cholly enters the kitchen intending to rape Pecola.

____ 10. Cholly lives with Uncle O.V. after Aunt Jimmy dies.

Write brief answers to the following questions.

11. Why does Mr. MacTeer shoot at Mr. Henry?

12. Why do Claudia and Frieda go to Pecola's house?

13. How does Pecola's mother react when Pecola knocks the berry cobbler to the floor?

14. Identify two reasons the Breedlove's marriage deteriorates.

15. What effect does Mrs. Breedlove's work for the Fisher family have on her?

16. What happens when Cholly and Darlene are sexually involved?

17. Give two facts about Soaphead Church.

18. What happened to Soaphead's mother?

19. Why does Pecola come to see Soaphead?

20. Why does Soaphead write a letter to God?

© Novel Units, Inc.   All rights reserved

Name _____

The Bluest Eye
Activity #20 • Quiz 4
Use After Reading Pages 187–216

Directions: Match each phrase with the correct character. You will need to use some characters more than once.

____ 1. Try to make a miracle by planting marigold seeds

____ 2. Has raped his daughter

____ 3. React to the rape with disgust and skepticism

____ 4. A brother who leaves

____ 5. Has a baby who dies

____ 6. Bases the novel on a personal experience

____ 7. Develops a hallucinatory other self

____ 8. Dies in the workhouse

____ 9. Beats her daughter after the rape

____ 10. Promises Pecola that her blue eyes will last forever

____ 11. Never go to see Pecola because of a sense of failure

____ 12. Searches the garbage

A. Pecola Breedlove

B. Frieda and Claudia

C. Sammy Breedlove

D. Soaphead Church

E. Toni Morrison

F. Cholly Breedlove

G. Pauline Breedlove

H. Lorain townspeople

Name _____

The Bluest Eye
Final Test • Level One

A. Identification: Match each character with the correct identification. (1 pt. each)

____ 1. Pecola Breedlove   a. authoritative mother figure; helps Pecola
____ 2. Cholly Breedlove   b. fat; hates men; cares for Pecola
____ 3. Pauline Breedlove   c. hopeless, rejected child who searches for beauty
____ 4. Geraldine   d. lewd, charming boarder
____ 5. Claudia MacTeer   e. dysfunctional, alcoholic father
____ 6. Frieda MacTeer   f. manipulative, psychic, pedophile
____ 7. Mrs. MacTeer   g. cares more for employers' family than her own
____ 8. Mr. Henry   h. perceptive, bright, caring, narrator
____ 9. Miss Marie   i. bold, loyal, older sister of narrator
____ 10. Soaphead Church   j. mannerly, moral, passionless mother

B. Multiple Choice: Choose the best answer. (2 pts. each)

_____ 11. The phrase, "Quiet as it's kept, there were no marigolds in the fall of 1941" foreshadows
   (a) the rape of Pecola Breedlove
   (b) a poor crop year
   (c) the death of Aunt Jimmy
   (d) the narrator's financial ruin

_____ 12. The MacTeer family is best described as
   (a) poor and unconcerned
   (b) apathetic and lazy
   (c) frugal and loving
   (d) incapable and unloving

_____ 13. Pecola comes to stay with the MacTeer family
   (a) as a welfare case who has no place to go
   (b) after her mother deserts the family
   (c) because her father beats her
   (d) after she runs away from home

Name _____

The Bluest Eye
Final Test • Level One
page 2

_____ 14. Claudia's reaction to her dolls indicates
   (a) her desire to be like them
   (b) anger toward Pecola
   (c) jealousy of Maureen
   (d) confusion over people's response to white children but not to her

_____ 15. Claudia and Frieda's reaction to Pecola's arrival is best described as
   (a) angry and anxious
   (b) pleased and hospitable
   (c) jealous and retaliatory
   (d) unconcerned and calm

_____ 16. The Breedloves live
   (a) in a lakefront home
   (b) with the MacTeer family
   (c) upstairs above the prostitutes
   (d) in a storefront home

_____ 17. Pecola reacts to her parents' fighting by
   (a) praying that God will make her father leave
   (b) running away with Sammy
   (c) praying that God will make her disappear
   (d) going to the MacTeers' home

_____ 18. Pauline Breedlove assumes a martyr syndrome in order to
   (a) endure her marriage
   (b) endure her poverty
   (c) get government aid
   (d) retaliate against her children

_____ 19. To cover his own feelings of self-hatred, Cholly Breedlove
   (a) beats his children
   (b) divorces his wife
   (c) kills a white man
   (d) drinks

Name _____

The Bluest Eye
Final Test • Level One
page 3

_____ 20. Which of the following reflects the attitude of the three prostitutes?
    (a) hate all men and all women
    (b) hate men and respect some women
    (c) love men and hate women
    (d) hate some men and respect all women

_____ 21. Which of the following typifies the Breedloves' marriage?
    (a) love growing stronger
    (b) love turned to disgust
    (c) marriage of convenience
    (d) forced marriage

_____ 22. Because of her mother's reaction to her, Pecola
    (a) is filled with self-confidence
    (b) knows she is loved
    (c) hates her mother
    (d) believes she is ugly

_____ 23. Mrs. Breedlove's employment with the Fishers
    (a) supplies her family with luxuries
    (b) makes her hate her employers
    (c) causes her to view her own home and family unfavorably
    (d) causes her to view her own home and family more favorably

_____ 24. All but which one of the following is true of Cholly's background?
    (a) His mother abandons him.
    (b) He deserts Darlene because she is pregnant.
    (c) His father rejects him.
    (d) White men humiliate him.

_____ 25. The women attribute Aunt Jimmy's death to
    (a) pneumonia
    (b) bad apples
    (c) lack of care
    (d) peach cobbler

Name _____

The Bluest Eye
Final Test • Level One
page 4

_____ 26. Mr. Yacobowski treats Pecola with
    (a) respect
    (b) contempt
    (c) consideration
    (d) admiration

_____ 27. Pecola is harassed by a group of boys with taunts about
    (a) her color and her father
    (b) her ugliness and her brother
    (c) her color and her mother
    (d) her poverty and her friends

_____ 28. Maureen Peal is best characterized as
    (a) beautiful and compassionate
    (b) ugly but kind
    (c) captivating but cruel
    (d) silly but smart

_____ 29. Maureen makes Claudia and Frieda feel
    (a) hated
    (b) inadequate
    (c) loved
    (d) beautiful

_____ 30. Mr. Henry explains the prostitutes' presence in the MacTeers' home by saying
    (a) they are his sisters
    (b) they have come to see Mrs. MacTeer
    (c) he is helping them learn to read
    (d) they are members of his Bible class

_____ 31. Geraldine's relationship with her son Junior is best described as
    (a) aloof and unaffectionate
    (b) warm and affectionate
    (c) loving and concerned
    (d) unconcerned but loving

© Novel Units, Inc.   All rights reserved

Name _____

The Bluest Eye
Final Test • Level One
page 5

_____ 32. Junior entices Pecola into his house with
   (a) the promise to show her his kittens
   (b) a request for her help with the cat
   (c) an offer of cake and ice cream
   (d) the promise to let her play with his toys

_____ 33. Geraldine retaliates against Pecola because
   (a) Pecola hit Junior
   (b) Pecola screams at her
   (c) she believes Pecola killed her cat
   (d) she is angry at Mrs. Breedlove

_____ 34. Mr. MacTeer beats up Mr. Henry because
   (a) he won't pay the rent
   (b) he invites the prostitutes for a visit
   (c) he makes sexual advances toward Mrs. MacTeer
   (d) he makes sexual advances toward Frieda

_____ 35. When Pecola accidentally knocks the berry cobbler off the kitchen counter, Mrs. Breedlove
   (a) makes her clean it up
   (b) knocks her down
   (c) blames Frieda
   (d) blames the Fisher child

_____ 36. Pauline Breedlove attributes the loss of her dream to
   (a) her lame foot
   (b) her poverty
   (c) Cholly's inadequacies
   (d) her lack of education

_____ 37. Cholly rapes Pecola because
   (a) he has planned it for days
   (b) he wants to punish her for disobedience
   (c) Pauline has been taunting him
   (d) she reminds him of the young Pauline

Name _____

The Bluest Eye
Final Test • Level One
page 6

_____ 38. Soaphead Church proclaims himself to be
   (a) a minister of the Gospel
   (b) a medical doctor and psychic
   (c) a spiritualist and psychic reader
   (d) a teacher and healer

_____ 39. Soaphead's perversion involves
   (a) little boys
   (b) little girls
   (c) prostitutes
   (d) older women

_____ 40. After Pecola asks Soaphead to give her blue eyes, he manipulates her into
   (a) coming to live with him
   (b) bringing Claudia back with her
   (c) killing Bertha
   (d) killing a dog

_____ 41. Soaphead sums up his frustration with life by
   (a) writing a letter to his grandfather
   (b) writing a letter to God
   (c) writing a newspaper article
   (d) writing a novel

_____ 42. Which of the following indicates the result of Pecola's visit to Soaphead?
   (a) She will have blue eyes that only she can see.
   (b) She knows she will never have blue eyes.
   (c) She no longer wants blue eyes.
   (d) She realizes her own eyes are beautiful.

_____ 43. Which of the following does NOT reflect the community's attitude regarding Pecola's rape?
   (a) Pecola carries some of the blame.
   (b) Pecola carries none of the blame.
   (c) The child will be ugly if it lives.
   (d) Pecola has always been foolish.

Name _____

The Bluest Eye
Final Test • Level One
page 7

_____ 44. Claudia and Frieda decide to "make a miracle" by all but which one of the following?
(a) They promise to be good for a month.
(b) They give up their dreams of a bicycle.
(c) They give Pecola the money they have made selling seeds.
(d) They plant the marigold seeds.

_____ 45. Pecola's conversation about her blue eyes is indicative of
(a) her dreams of a better life
(b) her anger toward Claudia
(c) her family's insanity
(d) her own insanity

_____ 46. Which is NOT true in the denouement?
(a) Cholly dies in the workhouse.
(b) Sammy runs away.
(c) Pecola regains her sanity.
(d) Claudia and Frieda never visit with Pecola.

_____ 47. Toni Morrison wrote *The Bluest Eye*
(a) because she wanted blue eyes
(b) as a tribute to her sister
(c) because she overhead an elementary child say she wanted blue eyes
(d) as a college writing assignment

C. Essay: Answer one of the following in a well-developed paragraph of at least five sentences. (10 pts.)

(a) Explain why the title is or is not appropriate for the novel.
(b) Explain how the theme of self-hatred is developed in the novel.
(c) State three circumstances that lead to Pecola's insanity and explain these circumstances.

D. Creative Response: Choose one of the following. (6 pts.)

(a) Write name poems for two of the following: Pecola, Geraldine, Claudia, Pauline, Cholly.
(b) Write a metaphor poem for Self-hatred.

Name _____

The Bluest Eye
Final Test • Level Two

A. Identification: Identify 2 characters who had a positive role in Pecola's life and name one thing he or she did to make Pecola's life better. (2 pts. each)

1. _____ _____
    _____

2. _____ _____
    _____

B. Identification: Identify 4 characters who had a negative role in Pecola's life and name one thing he or she did that lowered Pecola's self-esteem. (2 pts. each)

3. _____ _____   4. _____ _____
   _____ _____   _____ _____
   _____ _____   _____ _____

5. _____ _____   6. _____ _____
   _____ _____   _____ _____
   _____ _____   _____ _____

C. Multiple Choice: Choose the best answer. (2 pts. each)

_____ 7. The novel is written in a combination of what two styles?
   (a) narrative/second person
   (b) narrative/third person omniscient
   (c) second person/third person
   (d) narrative/second person

_____ 8. The MacTeer family is best described as
   (a) harsh, poor, unconcerned
   (b) apathetic, slovenly, brusque
   (c) poor, loving, frugal
   (d) incapable, poor, angry

_____ 9. Claudia and Frieda's reaction to Pecola's arrival is best described as
   (a) angry and anxious
   (b) pleased and hospitable
   (c) jealous and retaliatory
   (d) unconcerned and calm

Name _____

The Bluest Eye
Final Test • Level Two
page 2

_____ 10. The Breedloves' storefront home symbolizes
   (a) hope for a better future
   (b) rejection of the white man's world
   (c) hatred for the children
   (d) the hopelessness and decay of their lives

_____ 11. Which of the following does NOT add to the disintegration of the Breedloves' marriage?
   (a) loneliness
   (b) fantasy
   (c) murder
   (d) alcoholism

_____ 12. The names of the three prostitutes symbolize
   (a) their hatred of all men
   (b) the invasion of countries during WWII
   (c) the United States' invasion of China during WWII
   (d) Poland's invasion of Russia during WWII

_____ 13. Which of the following typifies the Breedloves' marriage?
   (a) love growing stronger
   (b) love turned to disgust
   (c) marriage of convenience
   (d) forced marriage

_____ 14. Mrs. Breedlove's employment at the Fishers
   (a) supplies her family with luxuries
   (b) makes her hate her employers
   (c) causes her to view her own home and family unfavorably
   (d) causes her to view her own home and family more favorably

_____ 15. Mrs. Breedlove instills in her children fear of all but which one of the following?
   (a) starvation
   (b) being clumsy
   (c) being like their father
   (d) not being loved by God

© Novel Units, Inc.   All rights reserved

Name _____

The Bluest Eye
Final Test • Level Two
page 3

_____ 16. All but which one of the following is true of Cholly's background?
  (a) His mother abandons him.
  (b) He deserts Darlene because she is pregnant.
  (c) His father rejects him.
  (d) White men humiliate him.

_____ 17. Junior's cruelty to the cat symbolizes his hatred for
  (a) all animals
  (b) his father
  (c) his mother
  (d) Pecola

_____ 18. Which one of the following is NOT true about Soaphead Church?
  (a) His father was a violent schoolmaster.
  (b) He abandoned his wife.
  (c) His wife left him after two months of marriage.
  (d) He experiences pedophiliac desires.

_____ 19. After Pecola asks Soaphead to give her blue eyes, he manipulates her into
  (a) coming to live with him
  (b) bringing Claudia back with her
  (c) killing Bertha
  (d) killing Bob

_____ 20. Which of the following indicates the result of Pecola's visit to Soaphead?
  (a) She will have blue eyes that only she can see.
  (b) She knows she will never have blue eyes.
  (c) She no longer wants blue eyes.
  (d) She realizes her own eyes are beautiful.

_____ 21. Which of the following does NOT reflect the community's attitude toward Pecola's rape?
  (a) Pecola carries some of the blame.
  (b) Pecola carries none of the blame.
  (c) The child will be ugly if it lives.
  (d) Pecola has always been foolish.

Name _____

The Bluest Eye
Final Test • Level Two
page 4

_____ 22. Claudia and Frieda decide to "make a miracle" by all but which of the following?
   (a) promising to be good for a month
   (b) giving up their dreams of a bicycle
   (c) giving Pecola the money they have made selling seeds
   (d) planting the marigold seeds

_____ 23. Pecola's remaining fear is
   (a) that her eyes are not the bluest
   (b) that she will lose her blue eyes
   (c) that no one will believe she did not encourage her father's sexual advances
   (d) that she will never be able to return to school

_____ 24. Toni Morrison wrote *The Bluest Eye*
   (a) because she wanted blue eyes
   (b) as a tribute to her sister
   (c) because she overhead an elementary child say she wanted blue eyes
   (d) as a college writing assignment

D. Short Answer: Write brief answers to the following questions. (2 pts. each)

25. What does the phrase, "As quiet as it's kept, there were no marigolds in the fall of 1941" foreshadow?
26. Why does Pecola come to stay with the MacTeer family?
27. What does Claudia's reaction to her dolls indicate?
28. Describe Maureen Peal and explain how she affects Pecola, Claudia, and Frieda.
29. What does Pecola symbolize to Geraldine?
30. How does Pecola react to her parents' fighting?
31. Contrast the way Mrs. Breedlove treats Pecola with the way she treats the Fishers' child.
32. How does Geraldine mold the character of her son, Junior?
33. Explain the circumstances that lead Cholly to rape Pecola.
34. What does Soaphead Church proclaim himself to be?
35. Why does Soaphead write a letter to God?

Name _____

The Bluest Eye
Final Test • Level Two
page 5

36. What does Pecola's conversation about her blue eyes indicate?
37. Explain what happens to the following characters in the denouement: Cholly, Sammy, Pecola, Claudia.

E. Literary Terms: Correctly identify the following literary devices. (2 pts. each)

38. _____ Winter moves into Mr. MacTeer's face.
39. _____ Maureen's legs look like dandelion stems.
40. _____ reference to Dante's Beatrice
41. _____ Men clustered like grapes.
42. _____ Elihue's mind was a soundless cave.

F. Essay: Choose one of the following and respond in a well-developed paragraph of at least seven sentences. (10 pts.)

(a) Explain the cycle of rejection that culminates in Pecola Breedlove's insanity.

(b) Explain the relationship of the excerpts from the Dick and Jane primer to the events in the novel.

(c) Explain how racial hatred manifests itself in Maureen Peal, Geraldine, Mr. Yacowboski, and Soaphead Church.

G. Creative Response: Choose one of the following. (6 pts.)

(a) Write a diamente poem contrasting Self-hate with Self-acceptance.

(b) Write a rap or a song that characterizes Cholly Breedlove.

(c) Write a five-senses poem about Rejection.

Answer Key

Activities #1 & #2: Responses will vary. **Activity #3:** 1. cheerfulness; others indicate sorrow. 2. vigorous; others refer to characteristics of old age. 3. inside; others refer to outer edge. 4. blithe; others indicate sorrow. 5. bland; others mean something sharp. 6. recent; others refer to something original. 7. altruism; others indicate hostility. 8. dialogues; others indicate one speaker. 9. unrepentant; others relate to being shamed. 10. contradiction; others mean proof. 11. straightforward; others indicate deceit. 12. overtness; others mean something hidden. 13. energy; others refer to lack of energy. 14. satisfaction; others indicate lack of satisfaction. 15. restoration; others mean to destroy. 16. verbal; others mean unspoken. 17. explainable; others relate to something that cannot be expressed. 18. amiable; others indicate irritability. 19. oversights; others indicate acknowledgement. 20. manifest; others mean hidden.
Activity #4: 1. extemporized 2. unabashed 3. macabre 4. gelid 5. ashen 6. epiphany 7. surfeit 8. inviolable 9. mulatto 10. genuflected **Activity #5:** Charts will vary. Example—Word: furtive; Synonyms: secretive, stealthy, sly, hidden; Antonyms: honest, open, upright, virtuous; Definition in own words: to do something secretly or to deceive by hiding one's actions from others; Used in a sentence: The store manager alerted security because of the man's furtive manner. **Activity #6:** 1. d 2. h 3. f 4. e 5. j 6. a 7. b 8. g 9. i 10. c

Study Guide—Preface–page 32: 1. Pecola: black child who is pregnant with her father's child; the child dies. Claudia MacTeer: narrator, both as a child and an adult, 9 years old; black. Frieda MacTeer: Claudia's 11-year-old sister. Cholly Breedlove: Pecola's father who rapes her; Mrs. MacTeer: Claudia and Frieda's mother 2. with a selection from the "Dick and Jane" reading primer; to contrast lifestyles of white and black children (preface) 3. because Pecola was having her father's baby; Only later could Claudia and Frieda admit their error and see that no seeds sprouted that year (p. 5). 4. Her father tried to burn up their house and she has nowhere to go; They are poor, and her father is an abusive alcoholic (pp. 16-17). 5. "outdoors," you have nowhere to go; "out," you have somewhere to go (p. 17) 6. She hates them and wants to dismember them, breaking off their fingers, loosening their hair, and removing their eyes to try to find the source of their desirability (pp. 19-23). 7. Pecola begins her menstrual periods; The MacTeer sisters try to help Pecola by cleaning up the blood and getting her a protective pad (pp. 27-28). 8. Activity **Pages 33–58:** 1. They live in an abandoned storefront that shows poverty in appearance and furnishings; Their lives are also decaying (pp. 34-35). 2. "They lived there because they were poor and black, and they stayed there because they believed they were ugly" (p. 38). 3. Mrs. Breedlove: as an actor does a prop, becoming a "martyr"; Sammy: as a weapon to cause others pain; Pecola: hides behind hers; Cholly: drinks (pp. 38-39) 4. to be used by God to punish Cholly for his sins (p. 42) 5. his drinking and her reaction to it; they need the fights to make their lives tolerable; Mrs. Breedlove because the lower he sinks, the more rewarding her task of redeeming him; Cholly because she is one of the few things he hates that he can touch and hurt; Sammy leaves the house or joins in the fighting; Pecola endures (pp. 42-43) 6. ugly, ignored, despised; teachers and classmates ignore her, she sits alone at a double desk, and classmates use her to insult boys. Mr. Yacobowski treats her with contempt, as if she isn't even there and is not worth noticing (pp. 45-49). 7. to have blue eyes; thinks this will make her beautiful and make everything all right (pp. 46-47) 8. She thinks she owns them and that makes her part of the world and the world part of her (pp. 47-48). 9. prostitutes: China, Poland, Miss Marie (the Maginot Line); older women, have many boyfriends, laugh often, hate men and respect only good Christian colored women; Pecola finds refuge with them, and they welcome her (pp. 52-58). 10. Activity **Pages 61–80:** 1. new student, a "high-yellow" child who has money and beautiful clothes; captivates all black and white students and teachers (pp. 62-63) 2. The boys surround her, taunt her that she is black and her father sleeps naked; Pecola is afraid, cries, drops her notebook, and covers her eyes with her hands; Frieda stops them by yelling at them and threatening to tell what one boy has done (pp. 65-66) 3. joins the MacTeer girls in rescuing Pecola; initially befriends Pecola but ignores the other two; tries to find out if boy's taunts about Pecola's father are true; gets into argument with the girls and begins to taunt and reject Pecola (pp. 66-73) 4. fascinated and irritated; jealous of her but secretly would like to be her friend; The "Thing" is whatever makes Maureen, but not them, beautiful (pp. 63-64, 74). 5. China and Miss Marie (the Maginot Line); says they are members of his Bible class who have come to read scriptures with him (pp. 77-79) 6. Their mother vows she will never allow the Maginot Line to eat from one of her plates, and she hasn't done that, so they don't tell their mother (pp. 77-79). 7. Activity 8. Activity **Pages 81–93:** 1. Geraldine typifies a well-mannered, morally pure, thrifty, and passionless black woman who despises blacks who do not live up to her standards; nice, well-kept home, well-cared for but not loved child, loves her cat (pp. 81-86) 2. takes care of him physically but does not talk to him or show him affection; loves her cat more than Junior; he hates her and takes out his hatred on the cat; significant because he finally kills the cat and blames it on Pecola (pp. 86-91) 3. He refuses to allow her to leave and shuts her up in a room but becomes enraged when she pets the cat; The cat is killed when he and Pecola struggle; Junior tells his mother that Pecola killed the cat, and Geraldine becomes violently angry at her. Pecola is terrified and feels worse than ever about herself (pp. 88-93). 4. Activity **Pages 97–109:** 1. Mr. Henry fondles Frieda's breasts; Her father attacks Mr. Henry, fires a gun at him, and forces him to run away (pp. 97-102). 2. Miss Dunion mentions that Frieda might be ruined, causing her to fear becoming fat like the "ruined" prostitute; they decide Frieda needs to drink whiskey to keep her from getting fat like the Maginot Line, so they go to Pecola's house since Cholly drinks and will have whiskey (pp. 101-103). 3. Pecola accidentally knocks the berry cobbler to the floor; Pecola's mother knocks her to the floor and screams at her to get out; She lovingly consoles the Fisher child (pp. 107-109). 4. Activity 5. Activity **Pages 110–131:** 1. childhood injury leaves her with a lame foot which she thinks causes the death of her dreams; she loves to arrange things neatly; takes care of younger siblings; dreams of someone who will rescue her (pp. 110-114) 2. symbolically: the "Presence" who will take her away from her monotonous life; reality: Cholly Breedlove, with whom she falls in love; He marries her and takes her away but the marriage disintegrates (pp. 114-115). 3. In the beginning the Breedloves are in love, happy, and excited about their future; Pauline becomes dissatisfied, lonely, and too dependent on Cholly; He resents her and begins to drink. Their fights get more intense; her fantasies make her feel uglier and Cholly more undesirable (pp. 117-134). 4. fantasy: in movies, everyone is handsome and beautiful, plenty of money, beautiful homes, and attentive husbands; reality: Pauline is pregnant, loses a front tooth, Cholly drinks and isn't attentive; They fight all the time (pp. 122-123, 127-128). 5. when pregnant: planned pregnancy, pleased, talks to baby; after: baby looks different than Pauline thought, thinks Pecola is smart but ugly; Pecola grows up thinking she is ugly (pp. 124-126). 6. Activity **Pages 132–163:** 1. mother: abandons Cholly when he is four days old; father: leaves town before he is born; Great Aunt Jimmy: rescues, loves, raises him; Blue Jack: friendly, father figure, cares for him; After Aunt Jimmy dies, Cholly feels rejected and searches for love; doesn't know how to be a husband or a parent (pp. 132-161) 2. White men find and interrupt them, then force them to continue while the men watch; Cholly is humiliated and turns his hatred toward Darlene because she knows his weaknesses and he can't hate the white men (pp. 146-150). 3. search for his father; He doesn't want to live with his uncle and is afraid Darlene might be pregnant and her father will find him; thinks his father will understand (pp. 151-152) 4. finds him after several months; father is gambling and curses at Cholly; Feeling lonely and rejected, Cholly runs away (pp. 154-157). 5. She reminds him of Pauline when they first met (pp. 161-163). **Pages 164–183:** 1. West Indian by birth; grandfather a religious fanatic, father a violent schoolmaster, mother died soon after his birth, wife left him after two months of marriage; proclaims himself to be a spiritualist and psychic reader; has pedophiliac desires for little girls (pp. 164-173) 2. Bertha: Soaphead's landlady; Bob: her dog (pp. 171, 175) 3. He counsels people who come to him in dread, reflecting their anger, yearning, pride, vengeance, loneliness, misery, defeat, and hunger; They ask him for love, health, and money (p. 172). 4. He can solve people's troubles and unnatural conditions including spells, bad luck, and evil influences; promises satisfaction in one visit (p. 173) 5. wants him to give her blue eyes; Soaphead feels mixed emotions of love, understanding, and anger and wishes he could make a miracle for her; tells her to feed Bob (the dog) some food and, if the dog reacts, she will have her blue eyes; manipulates her into killing Bob because he hates the dog; Bob dies and Pecola thinks she has her blue eyes (pp. 173-174). 6. through a letter he writes to God (pp. 176-182) 7. She was his "Beatrice"; he loved her; she left him like people leave a hotel room and doesn't want to remember their life together;

feels she never really left him because she wasn't actually there (pp. 170, 177-178) 8. Activity
Pages 187–206: 1. Her father raped her, she is pregnant; the townspeople who discuss her think the baby will die, Cholly is crazy, Pecola is foolish, she should be removed from school because she carries some of the blame; The girls feel sorry for her and want the baby to live (pp. 188-189). 2. Claudia and Frieda give up dreams of a bicycle, bury the money they have made selling marigold seeds, and try to be good for a month; The girls plant the marigold seeds, thinking that if the seeds grow, Pecola's baby will live (pp. 191-192). 3. with her hallucinatory self; They discuss Pecola's blue eyes, and the other "self" keeps assuring Pecola that her eyes are blue; Pecola worries that her eyes might not be the bluest; conversation reveals that Cholly tried to or did rape Pecola at least one other time (pp. 193-204) 4. At first they see her sometimes but later they stay away from her because they think they failed her since the marigolds didn't sprout (pp. 204-205). 5. Activity 6. Activity **Pages 209–216:** 1. She overheard an elementary student say she wished she had blue eyes and wants to reveal the destructiveness of the girl's racial self-hatred. 2. Responses will vary. 3. Activity

Note: Responses to activities will vary. This key offers suggested answers.
Activity #7: Pecola; Acts: intimidated, afraid, lonely; Says: she wants blue eyes, asks how you get someone to love you, denies her father sleeps naked, converses with self about her blue eyes; Feels About Self: ugly, worth nothing; Others' Attitudes: except for MacTeer family and the prostitutes, others act as if she isn't there or as if she is not worth anything; Looks: ugly (by others' standards), poor, subdued; Saddest Quote: Will you come back if I get them (the bluest eyes)? **Activity #8:** Cholly Breedlove; Statements: My name is Cholly (to father). Leave me alone (to Pauline, indicating his withdrawal as husband and father); Behavior: shiftless, drinks, fights with his wife, rapes daughter; Fears: white men, humiliation; Thoughts: his need to escape and find his father, how beautiful and perfect Pauline is (at first); how much he hates her (later); how much he hates Darlene for knowing about his weaknesses and the white men for humiliating him; how much Pecola reminds him of Pauline; Looks: tall, black, strong (when he meets Pauline); dejected and beaten down (later); Others' Actions: lack of respect, rejection, hatred, fear (his children).
Activity #9: Pecola: fearful, self-hatred, ashamed, longs for blue eyes; Claudia: bright, caring, sensitive, rejects white standards of beauty; Mrs. MacTeer: protective, loving but not indulgent, authoritative; Pauline Breedlove: feels ugly because of lame foot, harsh and abusive toward family, ideal employee, vindictively religious; Cholly Breedlove: slothful, abusive, alcoholic, rejected from childhood; Soaphead Church: town psychic, pedophile, manipulative, melancholy; Maureen Peal: mulatto child, has money and beautiful clothes, captivating but cruel; Geraldine: mannerly, moral, passionless, disdainful of poor blacks, loves cat more than son; Louis Junior: cruel, vindictive, prejudiced. **Activity #10:** Center: Pecola—ugly, fearful, inhibited, unloved; Circles: Cholly—abusive, alcoholic, slothful; interaction with Pecola: she fears him and longs for his love, he feels mixture of hate and tenderness; feels guilty because he hasn't taken care of Pecola; ultimately rapes her; Mrs. Breedlove—lonely, abusive, neglectful; interaction: Pecola longs for her love and approval; her mother neglects her and fails to show her love and understanding; Soaphead Church—psychic, pedophile, manipulative; interaction: Pecola asks him to give her blue eyes; he manipulates her and promises what he cannot give; convinces her she has blue eyes; Miss Marie—prostitute, fat, hates men; interaction: Pecola feels welcome and takes refuge with her; Miss Marie gives her a place of refuge and makes her feel wanted. **Activity #11:** Victims: Pecola, Cholly, Pauline, Sammy, Soaphead, Junior. Victimizers: Cholly, Pauline, Sammy, Soaphead, Junior, Geraldine, Mr. Henry, Mr. Yacobowski, Maureen Peal. Fighters: Sammy, Cholly, Pauline, Louis. Peace-lovers: Pecola, Claudia, Frieda, Mr. and Mrs. MacTeer, the three prostitutes, Aunt Jimmy. Conformists: Pecola, Aunt Jimmy, Geraldine, Darlene. Self-directors: Claudia, Frieda, Pauline, Mrs. MacTeer, Geraldine, Soaphead.
Activity #12: Characters: The Breedlove family (Pecola, Pauline, Cholly, Sammy), the MacTeer family (Claudia, Frieda, their parents), Soaphead Church, Geraldine, Junior, the three prostitutes, Mr. Henry. Setting: Lorain, Ohio, early 1940s. Themes: self-hatred, rejection, racism, survival. Conflict: self vs. self, family conflict, race vs. race. Genre: fiction. Point of View: first-person and third-person omniscient. Author's Style and Tone: narrative, omniscient voice, stream-of-consciousness.

Activity #13: 1. The narrator reveals that Pecola is raped by her father and her baby dies. Other events occur as flashbacks. 2. Pecola comes to stay with the MacTeer family because her father tries to burn up their house. The Breedlove family is dysfunctional with the parents fighting and not caring for the children. 3. Pecola is mistreated by a group of boys who torment her, by Maureen Peal, who befriends, then rejects her, and by Geraldine and Junior, who are vicious and drive her away from their home. 4. Cholly rapes Pecola and Soaphead promises her blue eyes. 5. Pecola becomes "mad" and invents a hallucinatory friend who talks to her about her blue eyes. **Activity #14:** Theme: self-hatred. Spokes: rejection, fear, intimidation, manipulation, generational, withdrawal, dream of better things, destruction.

Activity #15, Part 1: Events: 1. Cholly Breedlove is abandoned and rejected by his parents (C). 2. Cholly and Pauline fall in love and marry, but their marriage disintegrates (C, E). 3. Pecola is born and her mother thinks she is ugly (C). 4. Pecola prays for blue eyes (E). 5. Pecola's father tries to burn up their house (C, E). 6. Pecola stays with the MacTeers because she has nowhere else to go (E). 7. Children, teachers, her mother, Geraldine and Junior ignore, reject, and mistreat Pecola (C, E). 8. Cholly rapes Pecola (C, E). 9. Soaphead manipulates Pecola into thinking she has blue eyes (C, E). 10. Pecola's baby dies and she goes insane (E). **Part 2:** Causes: 1. Pecola's mother thinks she is ugly and neglects her. 2. Children and teachers ignore and taunt Pecola. 3. Geraldine and Junior treat Pecola viciously. 4. Cholly rapes Pecola. Effect: Pecola suffers from self-hatred and longs to have blue eyes so she will be beautiful and loved.

Activity #16: Result: Pecola goes insane, conversing with a hallucinatory friend about Pecola's blue eyes. Causes and Details: 1. She lacks a loving home environment. Her parents fight and Pecola prays that she will disappear. Her mother thinks she is ugly and prefers her employers' white child to Pecola. She instills numerous fears in Pecola. 2. Pecola feels unwanted at school and everywhere else. Teachers ignore her, students use her to taunt others, Mr. Yacobowski treats her with contempt, and Maureen rejects her. 3. Cholly rapes her. He is drunk, and she reminds him of Pauline when she was younger. She is pregnant with his child, who is born too soon and dies. 4. Soaphead Church promises her she will have blue eyes. He manipulates her into killing a dog. He tells God in a letter that Pecola will have blue eyes only she can see.

Activity #17, Quiz 1: 1. F (pp. 10-12, 31-32) 2. T (pp. 19-21) 3. F (pp. 27-30) 4. F (pp. 43-46) 5. T (pp. 48-50) 6. T (pp. 55-56) 7. Pecola is having her father's baby (preface) 8. her father tried to burn up their house; she has nowhere else to go (pp. 16-17). 9. Mr. Henry (pp. 12-15) 10. she has blue eyes (p. 46) 11. China, Poland, Miss Marie (the Maginot Line) (pp. 50-51) **Activity #18, Quiz 2:** 1. Maureen Peal (pp. 62, 67-73) 2. China and Miss Marie (or the Maginot Line) (pp. 77-78) 3. Geraldine (pp. 81-86) 4. on the playground (p. 88) 5. all the poor little black girls she has ever known (pp. 91-92) 6. surround her, taunt her with references to her color and her daddy's sleeping naked (pp. 65-66) 7. takes care of him physically but doesn't talk to him, cuddle him, or play with him (p. 86) 8. His mother loves the cat more than she loves him; He directs his hatred for his mother toward the cat (p. 86). 9. He invites her in to see kittens, throws the cat at her, refuses to let her leave, then accidently kills the cat and blames Pecola (pp. 88-91). 10. says they're members of his Bible class who have come to read scriptures with him (p. 78) **Activity #19, Quiz 3:** 1. F (pp. 108-109) 2. T (p. 110) 3. T (pp. 115-116) 4. F (p. 126) 5. T (p. 123) 6. F (pp. 129-131) 7. T (pp. 132-138) 8. T (pp. 151-156) 9. F (pp. 161-163) 10. F (pp. 151-153) 11. because Mr. Henry makes sexual advances toward Frieda (pp. 98-100) 12. to get some whiskey (p. 101) 13. knocks her down, screams at her, tells her to leave (pp. 108-109) 14. Responses will vary. For example—loneliness, disinterest, alcoholism, fantasy, dissatisfaction (pp. 117-121) 15. makes her more dissatisfied with her own life; neglects own family and home (pp. 127-129) 16. white men interrupt them, make them continue while they watch, humiliate Cholly (pp. 147-149) 17. West Indian by birth, violent father, wife left him after two months, pedophile, claims to be spiritualist and psychic reader (pp. 164-172) 18. died shortly after his birth (p. 169) 19. to ask him to give her blue eyes (p. 174) 20. to complain about God's actions and explain why Soaphead is like he is (pp. 176-182) **Activity #20, Quiz 4:** 1. B (p. 188) 2. F (pp. 198-199) 3. H (p. 190) 4. C (pp. 200-201) 5. A (p. 204) 6. E (p. 209) 7. A (pp. 193-204) 8. F (p. 205) 9. G (p. 189) 10. D (p. 193) 11. B (pp. 204-205) 12. A (p. 206)

Final Tests
Level One: A. 1. c 2. e 3. g 4. j 5. h 6. i 7. a 8. d 9. b 10. f **B.** 11. a (preface) 12. c (pp. 9-12, 23-25, 31-32) 13. a (pp. 16-19) 14. d (pp. 19-23) 15. b (19) 16. d (pp. 38-39) 17. c (pp. 44-45) 18. a (pp. 40-43) 19. d (pp. 42-43) 20. b (p. 56) 21. b (pp. 117-131) 22. d (pp. 123-126) 23. c (pp. 126-128) 24. b (pp. 132, 147-149, 156-157) 25. d (pp. 135, 139) 26. b (pp. 48-49) 27. a (pp. 65-67) 28. c (pp. 62-63, 71-73) 29. b (p. 74) 30. d (p. 78) 31. a (pp. 86-88) 32. a (pp. 88-89) 33. c (pp. 91-92) 34. d (pp. 97-100) 35. b (pp. 108-109) 36. a (pp. 110-111) 37. d (pp. 161-163) 38. c (p. 173) 39. b (pp. 166, 178-179) 40. d (pp. 173-176) 41. b (pp. 176-182) 42. a (pp. 181-182) 43. b (pp. 188-190) 44. c (pp. 191-192) 45. d (pp. 193-204) 46. c (pp. 204-205) 47. c (pp. 209-210) **C & D.** Responses will vary.

Level Two: A. 1-2: Responses will vary but may include Mr. and Mrs. MacTeer, Claudia and Frieda: her friends, welcome her into their home and take care of her; any of the three prostitutes, China, Poland, Miss Marie: are friendly and welcome her to their home. **B.** 3-6: Responses will vary but may include Cholly: drinks, making her afraid, rapes her; Mrs. Breedlove: ignores her, thinks she is ugly, prefers employers' child over her own; Maureen Peal: befriends, then rejects her; Mr. Yacobowski: treats her with contempt; Geraldine: vicious and cruel to her; Soaphead Church: lies to her, manipulates her. **C.** 7. b 8. c (pp. 9-12, 23-25, 31-32) 9. b (p. 19) 10. d (pp. 38-39) 11. c (pp. 117-126) 12. b (pp. 50-58, inference) 13. b (pp. 117-131) 14. c (pp. 126-128) 15. a (p. 128) 16. b (pp. 132, 147-149, 156-157) 17. c (p. 86) 18. b (pp. 164-171) 19. d (pp. 173-176) 20. a (pp. 181-182) 21. b (pp. 188-190) 22. c (pp. 191-192) 23. a (pp. 203-204) 24. c (pp. 209-210) **D.** 25. Pecola's rape by her father (preface) 26. Her father tries to burn the house down and she has nowhere else to go (pp. 16-19). 27. The dolls are white, and she doesn't understand why people respond favorably to white children but not to her (pp. 19-23). 28. cute, captivating, "high-yellow dream child," beautiful clothes, wealthy; Claudia and Frieda jealous but secretly want to be her friend; befriends Pecola but then turns against her (pp. 62-73) 29. all the poor little black girls she's ever known (pp. 97-100) 30. prays that God will let her disappear (pp. 44-45) 31. Pecola: angry, abusive, uncaring; Fishers' child: loving, gentle, kind (pp. 108-109) 32. cares for him physically but gives no love; insists he must play only with white children; instills hatred for black people (pp. 86-88) 33. He is drunk and sees her in the kitchen; she reminds him of Pauline when they first met. She scratches the back of her leg with her toe as Pauline had done and he is filled with lust and tenderness for her (pp. 161-163). 34. spiritualist and psychic reader (p. 173) 35. to explain why Soaphead is attracted to little girls, to blame God for not taking care of important issues such as Velma's leaving, and because he thinks God hasn't done what He should have for Pecola (pp. 176-182) 36. She has, in her insanity, developed a hallucinatory friend to whom she can talk about her blue eyes (pp. 203-204). 37. Cholly dies in the workhouse; Sammy: leaves town; Pecola: becomes hallucinatory, roams around, digs in the garbage; Claudia: never goes near Pecola because she feels she failed her (pp. 204-206). **E.** 38. Personification (p. 61) 39. Simile (p. 73) 40. Allusion (pp. 169-170) 41. Simile (p. 154) 42. Metaphor (p. 170) **F & G.** Responses will vary.